GRANDMA MAXINE REMEMBERS

Text © 2002 by Ann Morris
Photographs and illustrations © 2002 by Peter Linenthal
Designed by Carolyn Eckert
Additional photographs courtesy of © Bettmann/Corbis: p. 18;
© George Robbins photo: p. 6; © the Wesaw family: pp.10, 14, 17, 19, 32

Library of Congress Cataloging-in-Publication Data

Morris, Ann, 1930-
Grandma Maxine remembers: a Native American family story/Ann Morris;
photographs and illustrations by Peter Linenthal.
p. cm. — (What was it like, Grandma?)
Summary: A Shoshone grandmother relates family and cultural history to
her granddaughter as they share their daily tasks on the Wind River Indian
Reservation in Wyoming. Includes a recipe, craft, and activities.
ISBN 0-7613-2317-1 (lib. bdg.)
1. Shoshoni girls—Social life and customs—Juvenile literature.
2. Shoshoni Indians—History—Juvenile literature.
3. Shoshoni Indians—Social life and customs—Juvenile literature.
4. Wind River Indian Reservation (Wyo.)—Social life and customs—
Juvenile literature.
5. Indian craft—Juvenile literature. [1. Shoshoni Indians. 2. Indians of
North America—Wyoming.
3. Wind River Indian Reservation (Wyo.)—Social life and customs. 4.
Indian craft.
5. Handicraft.] I. Linenthal, Peter, ill. II. Title.

E99.S4 M66 2002   978.004—9745—dc21   2001044087

The Millbrook Press, Inc.
2 Old New Milford Road
Brookfield, Connecticut 06804
All rights reserved
www.millbrookpress.com

Printed in Hong Kong
5 4 3 2 1

What Was It Like, Grandma?

GRANDMA MAXINE ✿ REMEMBERS

A Native American Family Story

Ann Morris

Photographs and illustrations by Peter Linenthal

The Millbrook Press
Brookfield, Connecticut

Shawnee is a Native American girl.

She belongs to the Shoshone tribe.

Shawnee lives in a house at Fort Washakie, Wyoming, on the Wind River Reservation. She lives with her mother, Wanda, one brother, two sisters, four dogs, and one cat. Her father, Marvin, lives in another town in Wyoming.

Shawnee's grandmother Maxine and her grandfather Pee Wee live nearby.

Shawnee with her Grandma Maxine

Romeo

Shawnee and Grandpa Pee Wee

Shawnee (left front), Sister Ashlee (right front), Cousin Amber (left back), Cousin Jessica (center back), Grandma Maxine (right back)

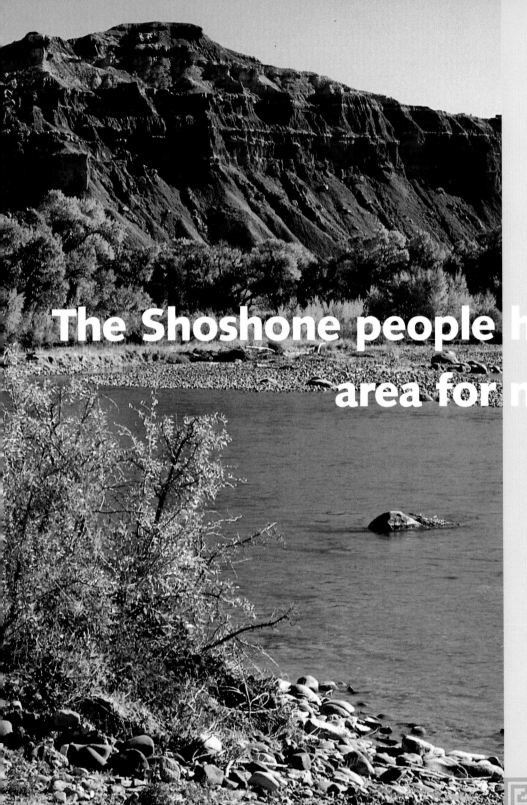

The Shoshone reservation covers more than two and a half million acres. It is one of the largest reservations for Native Americans in the United States.

The Shoshone people have lived in this area for many, many years.

It is a land of great beauty. It has mountains, streams, and lakes full of fish. Antelope, deer, and elk roam freely in the area. Buffalo also roam the reservation in fenced areas.

More than three thousand Shoshone people live on the reservation. Another group, the Arapaho, also live there.

Long ago the Shoshone people lived in tepees. Now they live in houses surrounded by land. They use tepees only for special occasions or celebrations.

Shawnee and Grandma Maxine walk on the land near their house.

Shawnee's house is close to the road.

Not far away are schools and grocery stores.

The family raises geese, ducks, chickens, and pigs for food.

They collect eggs for cooking and baking.

Shawnee likes to feed the geese and the pigs. The geese eat grain.

The pigs eat all kinds of leftover food.

Grandma Maxine

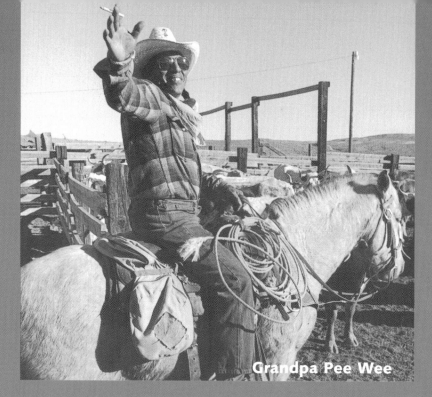

Grandpa Pee Wee

Grandma Maxine is a social worker.

She works in a Head Start center for young children. She helps parents make sure that their children get a healthy start in life.

Grandpa Pee Wee's real name is George.

He works on a nearby farm tending horses and rounding up cattle. Shawnee likes to walk to the fields near her house to pat the horses.

Shawnee and Grandma Maxine visit the horses.

Shawnee is in the third grade.
She goes to a school on the
reservation that is five miles away.
The school bus picks her up in
the morning and brings her home
in the afternoon.

Shawnee spends a lot of time
at her grandmother's house.
Sometimes they read together.
Sometimes they look at old
family photographs.

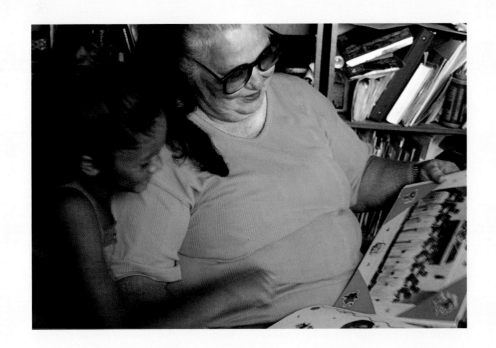

Maxine tells Shawnee stories about their family and the Shoshone people.

Shawnee likes to hear what things were like when Maxine and Pee Wee were little.

One of Maxine's grandmothers

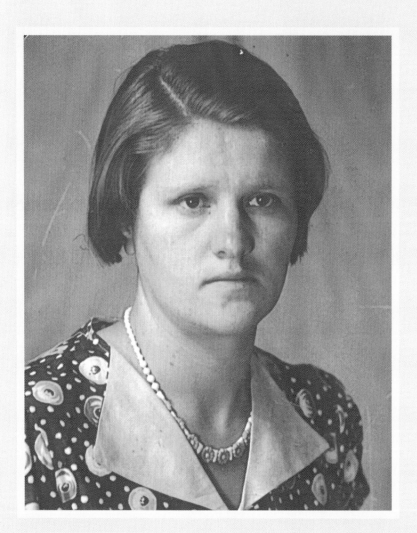

Maxine's mother

Grandma Maxine has lived on the reservation all her life and has only left it once to go to school.

When she was little, she lived with her mother, father, two sisters, two brothers, and one half brother. For a short time, one of her grandmothers also lived with the family.

In those days, there was only one school on the reservation. It was a two-room schoolhouse. Each day she and a brother walked five miles there and five miles back. When it snowed, her half brother would clear a trail so that the children could make their way through the snow.

Grandma Maxine tells Shawnee about all the chores that she had to do when she was young.

There was no running water in her house then.

Each day she had to get water from a well and carry it home.
The family heated water for their baths on a wood-burning stove.
Every day she and her sister milked four cows before leaving
for school. At night they drew straws to decide who would do the
dishes and who would feed the animals.

But there were fun times, too. In the
summer her family moved into the tepees.
Sometimes Maxine rode over the hills
on horseback with her cousins. They
also enjoyed making houses out of boxes
and playing in them. The children
played games that were like field hockey.
They called them "shinny" games
because when a player struck the ball, it
sometimes hit the shin of another player.

In winter the children made up their
own winter sports. They didn't have ice
skates, so they slid on the ice in their
shoes. They didn't have sleds, so they went
sliding down the hillside on plastic sheets.

Maxine and her sister, Alma Jean

Grandma Maxine also tells Shawnee about Grandpa Pee Wee's family.

Pee Wee is a descendant of Sacagawea, a famous Indian guide and interpreter.

Almost two hundred years ago, Sacagawea helped two famous explorers, Lewis and Clark, make their way across the rugged mountains and desert of the northwestern United States.

Pee Wee's father belonged to the War Bonnet Clan. He wore a beautiful headdress called a "war bonnet" that was made of eagle feathers.

Sacagawea on the Lewis and Clark Expedition

Pee Wee's mother carrying his little sister, Almona, in a cradleboard

Pee Wee's mother cared for the family. Like many Native American women, she carried her papooses—her babies— in a cradleboard on her back. Women did this to free their hands for work.

Pee Wee's father

Sometimes Shawnee and Grandma Maxine take long walks around the reservation. Out in the meadow, Maxine tickles Shawnee with wild sage. Sometimes Shawnee rubs its leaves in her hands. The strong smell helps keep the mosquitoes away.

Sage is often cooked with meat to give the meat a special flavor. Maxine tells Shawnee that the Shoshone people believe that sage is sacred and can clean the air and body. When the sage is used in ceremonies, its smell goes upward with the smoke and pleases the Creator.

Grandma Maxine places a wild rose in Shawnee's hair.

She tells her that the wild rose is a symbol of the Shoshone.

Often the wild rose design is used in Shoshone beadwork.

Long ago there were many wild roses on the reservation. In Shawnee's great-grandparents' time, the rose petals were used for making perfume.

There are many tepees on the Shoshone reservation, but they are used only on special ceremonial days and at powwows. Powwows are social gatherings where tribal people come together to trade, dance, and celebrate.

Grandma Maxine takes Shawnee to see a tepee. It probably belonged to a Shoshone chief. The tepee is made from canvas. It is warm and dry on the inside. There are furry rugs on the floor to sit on.

The tepee is decorated with the traditional markings of the Shoshone— hills, mountains, and buffalo.

Maxine tells Shawnee that buffalo are a symbol of strength. Once the buffalo roamed the area where the Shoshone live. The Shoshone used their hides to make clothes, blankets, and other things they needed. They used the buffalo meat for food.

"Sadly," Maxine says, "the buffalo nearly disappeared. Soldiers and hunters shot them long ago. But they are beginning to come back." The government now protects them. Only a few are killed each year to be used for food on special occasions.

Grandma Maxine teaches Shawnee tribal customs and dances.

Shawnee often performs the dances she learns at powwows. She wears moccasins—soft shoes made from elk or deer hide.

Sometimes Shawnee practices "fancy dancing" in the field in front of her house.

Pee Wee lets her wear his special belt made for the Sun Dance.

The belt is made of beads that Shawnee's great-aunt strung together on a loom. It took her two years to make it. Wild roses appear in the design.

Fry bread is a popular Native American food.

It is served at family gatherings, powwows, and other celebrations. It is also eaten at meals. Shawnee's family eats it with stew.

Shawnee likes to help Grandma Maxine make fry bread. She helps mix the dough and pat it into shapes— round, square, or triangular. Sometimes Shawnee does this too quickly.

Then Maxine says, "Take your time. When you rush through things, you rush through life and miss a lot." Shawnee understands and slows down. When she finishes forming the dough into shapes, her grandmother fries the pieces in oil.

As they make fry bread together, Maxine says, "You must cook with good feeling, or it won't turn out well. Bad feeling will go in the food."

Fry bread is fun to make and good to eat.

Fry Bread

Makes 10 or 12 fry breads.

Though each Native American group may make it somewhat differently, the basic ingredients for fry bread remain the same.

SAFETY TIP: If you try this, an adult should do the frying.

HERE IS WHAT YOU NEED:

3   cups unbleached flour

2   teaspoons baking powder

1   teaspoon salt

1½   cups warm water or milk

1   tablespoon vegetable oil or shortening

Oil or shortening for deep frying

HERE IS WHAT YOU DO:

1. Mix all the ingredients except the oil in a large bowl.

2. Knead the dough until it is nice and smooth.

3. Rub the tablespoon of oil over the dough.

4. Cover the bowl with a cloth and let the dough rise for about 30 minutes.

5. Uncover the bowl, take a handful of dough, and roll or pat it into a shape. The dough should be about ⅛ inch thick. Repeat until all the dough is used. You should have 10 to 12 pieces.

6. Heat the frying oil or shortening in a deep pan. When it is very hot (190°F), carefully place one piece of dough at a time in the oil and let it fry until it is puffy and crisp.

7. Place the finished pieces on paper towels to drain.

8. Serve the fry bread with honey or sprinkle with powdered sugar.

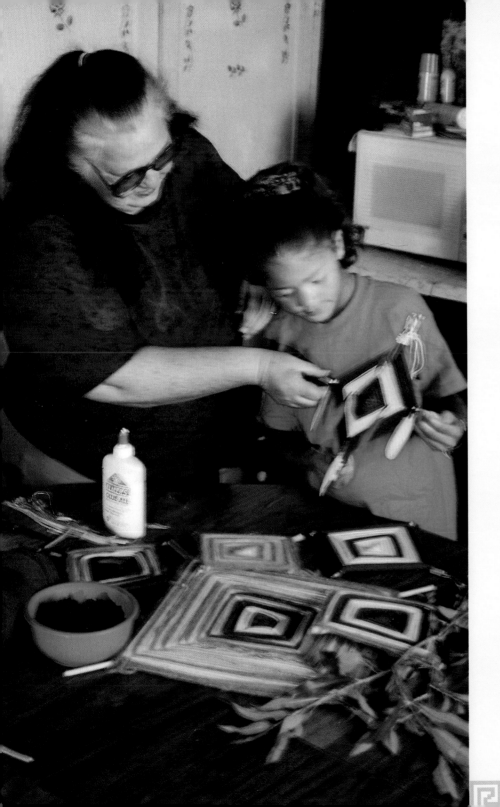

Sometimes Shawnee and Grandma Maxine make God's Eyes out of colorful pieces of yarn. A God's Eye is an ancient design from Mexico that was carried to Native Americans by traders and trappers.

Some people say God's Eyes are dream catchers.

They catch bad dreams and let good dreams go through. Some people believe they symbolize the four seasons. Other people believe God's Eyes express feelings. Maxine says the Shoshone people believe that God's Eyes bring good luck. They help make sure that children will have a long and healthy life.

God's Eyes

It is easy to make God's Eyes.

HERE IS WHAT YOU NEED:

String or yarn in several colors

Two ice cream or craft sticks

Glue

Scissors

HERE IS WHAT YOU DO:

1. Glue the two sticks together in the shape of a cross.

2. Let dry.

3. Take one color of yarn and tie it to the center of the cross.

4. Wrap the yarn under and around one stick, then under and around the next.

5. Pull the yarn tight and push it toward the center. Continue wrapping until you have as much of the color as you want.

6. Cut the yarn and tie on a different color yarn with a tight knot. Wrap it under and around the sticks as you did before.

7. Keep adding new yarn until your design reaches the end of the sticks.

8. After wrapping it under the stick for the last time, knot yarn to itself. Tie another knot to form a loop. Use the loop to hang the God's Eye in a window or on a wall.

ALL ABOUT MY FAMILY

Would you like to know about your family? Here are some things you can do.

INTERVIEWS

You will find out many interesting things about your relatives by interviewing them. Ask them questions about their childhood—where they lived, what they liked best to do and to eat, what they read and studied in school. Find out, too, how things are different today from when they were young. Use a tape recorder to record your questions and their answers.

FAMILY ALBUM

Ask your relatives for pictures of themselves. Put all the pictures in an album. Write something you have learned about each person under his or her picture.

FAMILY TREE

All of us have many relatives. Some of us are born into the family. Others are related by marriage or have been adopted. You can make a family tree that looks like the one on the next page to show who belongs to your family.

WESAW FAMILY TREE

Maxine

Pee Wee

Wanda

Marvin

Autumn

Ashlee

Shawnee

Darren

Romeo